FULL SAIL

John Wilson and Charles Rosamond

Oxford University Press
Music Department Walton Street Oxford OX2 6DP

3

MUSICAL
ALLSORTS

Teacher's notes

1 This book is designed to provide a term's work in music and related subject areas for a Middle Primary class.
2 The work could be covered by two 30 minute spells per week. This should be regarded as a minimum allocation.
3 A cassette accompanies the book and includes listening material and recordings of the songs. Simple guitar or piano accompaniments are provided on the cassette so that the melodic line can be heard clearly for teaching purposes. These should help the non pianist to teach the songs easily and quickly.
4 The songs should always be taught before the accompaniment is added.
5 Guitar chords are included and a chart showing chord positions and recorder notes is on page 30.
6 A variety of percussion instruments, tuned and untuned, is desirable. A list is included.
7 A list of records and books connected with the topic is provided.
8 An end performance of some kind is desirable and some suggestions are offered below.

Suggestions for end performance

1 The songs can be performed with or without accompaniment using the **narration** as linking material.
2 To this could be added some of the poems, dances, etc., created by the children.
3 The taped material may prove useful for linking, or as accompaniment for movement, etc.,
4 Simple costumes and 'props' could be made and used in the production.
5 A display of related art/craft work could be mounted.

List of desirable instruments

1 set chime bars and beaters   OR/AND
1 soprano glockenspiel   OR/AND
1 soprano xylophone
2 tambourines
1 drum or tambour
3 triangles
1 two tone block
yoghurt containers
4 – 6 recorders (descant)
1 large cymbal, padded stick and hard stick
1 cassette recorder
1 melodica or harmonica

Books for further reading

Sea Transport   D. Smith and D. Newton   (The *In History* series, Schofield and Sims)

Travel by Sea   Robert J. Hoare   (A. & C. Black)

Ships   Brian Benson   (Macdonald Visual Books)

Records for further listening

Sea Interludes from *Peter Grimes*   Britten   Decca SXL2189

Fingal's Cave   Mendelssohn   DG PRIV 2535/3335 460

Calm Sea and Prosperous Voyage   Mendelssohn   DG PRIV 2535/3335 460

La Mer   Debussy   HMV SXLP 30146

Portsmouth Point   Walton   HMV ASD 2990

Spartacus   Khachaturian . ASD 3347

Sheherazade   Rimsky-Korsakov   Philips 6500 410

Fantasia on British Sea Songs   Sir Henry Wood   FFM 23033

Pineapple Poll   Sullivan/Mackerras   HMV Greensleeves FSD 7028

Sea Dreams   MFP 41 56861

Introduction

My name is Karen Kelly, and I work in a shipping office. My great-grandfather was a sea captain, and I hope some day to follow in his footsteps by joining the W.R.N.S.* for a start, anyway!

In the meantime, I enjoy my job. There is always something interesting turning up. For instance, the other day I was helping to tidy away some old papers in a cupboard when my boss said 'Hold on Karen! Here's something that might interest you. These might tell you something about how your great-grandfather lived,' and he handed me a few yellowed sheets of paper. The boss was right. The papers <u>did</u> tell me something about what life must have been like in sailing ships. I thought they might be of interest to you too, so although many of the pages are missing, I am going to pass on to you the ones I have. I hope you find them as interesting as I did.

W.R.N.S.* – Women's Royal Naval Service.

Good morning ladies all

With a good swing

Now a long good – bye ____ to you, my dear, With a

heave Oh, haul ____ And a last fare – well and a

long fare – well, And good mor – ning la – dies all. ____

2 For we're outward bound to New York town,
  With a heave . . .
  And you'll wave to us till the sun goes down.
  And good morning . . .

3 And when we get to New York town,
  Oh it's there we'll drink, and sorrows drown.

4 When we're back once more in London Docks,
  All the pretty girls will come in flocks.

5 And Poll, and Bet, and Sue will say:
  'Oh it's here comes Jack with his three years' pay.'

6 So a long good-bye to you, my dear,
  And a last farewell, and a long farewell.

Some accompaniment ideas

RECORDER One or two recorders could play the melody line.

CHIME BARS Three players

Player 1 – needs

Player 2 – needs

Player 3 – needs

Setting sail

This was a big day for me. I travelled to Cardiff to join my ship, the '*Adventurer*'
I felt very proud of myself in my short, brass-bound jacket and the cap with the
badge that let the world know that I was a sailor – or anyway, a ship's apprentice,
earning £4 for my first year of service, and £9 for the fourth and final year – if I
lasted that long!

When I reached Cardiff, I had some difficulty finding the dock where the
'*Adventurer*' lay, for the port seemed to be full of ships, many of them steamships.
The year was 1902, and sail was fighting a losing battle with steam. At last I found
her – a beautiful full-rigged ship with three great masts, the tallest of which must
have been about 180 feet high. There was also a maze of rigging and ropes, about
which, at the moment I knew nothing.

I was met by the senior apprentice, Jim Short, who took me to see Captain
Macdonald. 'You've chosen a hard life, son. Think you're fit for it?' 'Y- y- yessir,' I
stammered. 'Fine then. Do your best at all times and obey orders. First order is,
get your working clothes on and give a hand shovelling coal. You'll have noticed
we're loading coal, and we're taking it to Peru. Off you go!'

Loading coal is hard, dirty work. Tonight I am really tired. I've washed off all –
or nearly all – the coal dust, and I'm ready for my bunk.

Creative ideas

Our friend is feeling really sleepy. How about trying to make up some sleepy
music?

Divide up into groups of four or five.
Decide on whether the music will be fast or slow or loud or quiet.

When you've made up your minds, find an instrument each – glockenspiels or
chime bars or any other quiet instruments would be useful.

Select the notes C D E G A and see if you can put together some 'sleepy' sounds
and make a 'sleepy' picture in sound. Remember you can use your voices and
perhaps some sleepy words!

LISTENING 1

Pineapple Poll: Opening dance

This music describes a busy quayside scene. It's full of movement and excitement. Can you visualize the scene: the ships with their tall masts and rigging, all the bustle of departure; people saying goodbye, loading cargo? Try to see this picture in your mind's eye as you listen. Listen once or twice and then try either to:

1 Paint the scene, *or*
2 Write a paragraph describing the scene in your own words, *or*
3 Compose a short poem describing the departure.
4 Can you find this tune?

Tell your teacher when you hear it!

Outward bound 20th May 1902

After two days loading coal and making things ship-shape, we were towed out of the harbour by a steam tug. Once clear of the harbour, we were ordered aloft to set the sails. First-year apprentices are not supposed to climb up the rigging, but we were sailing short-handed and everyone had to do his bit. Up the rigging I went, with no clear idea of what I had to do except to reach one of the yards. There I hung on like grim death and pretended to help. I suppose I shall learn in time, but the tangle of ropes and gear is a mystery. I shall also have to learn to hang on, as even in a fresh breeze the masts swing from side to side.

At last the job was done. The sails were broken out, the tug was left behind, and we were outward bound. The map on page 29 shows you our route to Peru.

As off to the South'ard we go

Cheerily

1. The wind is free and we're bound for sea, *Heave a-way cheer-i-ly ho, oh!* The las-ses are wav-ing to you and to me___ As off to the South'-ard we go___ *As off to the South'-ard we go.___ Sing my lads chee-ri-ly, heave my lads chee-ri-ly, Heave a-way chee-ri-ly, oh,___. For gold that we prize and sun-ni-er skies, A-way to the South'-ard we go.___*

2 They're waving good-bye and with tearful eye,
    Heave away cheerily, ho, oh!
Sing cheer up, my darlings, and wipe your tears dry,
    As off to the south'ard we go,
    As off to the south'ard we go.
    Sing, my lads, cheerily . . . .

3 They're crying, 'Come back, my dear Tom or dear Jack!'
  Heave away cheerily, ho, oh!
 There's water in front, and no door at the back,
  As off to the south'ard we go,
  As off to the south'ard we go,
   Sing, my lads, cheerily . . .

4 We want sailors bold, who can work for their gold,
  Heave away cheerily, ho, oh!
 And stand a good wetting without catching cold,
  As off to the south'ard we go,
  As off to the south'ard we go.
   Sing, my lads, cheerily . . .

5 The sailor is true to his Sal or his Sue,
  Heave away cheerily, ho, oh!
 As long as he's able to keep 'em in view,
  As off to the south'ard we go,
  As off to the south'ard we go.
   Sing, my lads, cheerily . . .

Some accompaniment ideas

DESCANT RECORDERS

Play the tune throughout.

TAMBOURINE AND DRUM (one each)
Play the rhythm of

Off to the south' – ard we go

every time these words appear.

CYMBAL

One clash on each of the following words marked with an ∗ on the opposite page.

∗ ∗
wind – bound
lass – you
gold – prize
sun – skies

GLOCKENSPIELS OR CHIME BARS

You will need three chords.

Play where named.

Jasper's solo

1 Which of the three pictures described below do you think is best illustrated by this music?

a Our friend asleep on his back.
b His new ship, all her sails set, sailing proudly along.
c Mischievous boys on the quayside turning and darting about.

2 Get into your groups again and discuss your selection. Try to decide why you have selected a particular picture.
Choose *six* words which would best describe this piece of music.
Make up a list of them in your notebook.

Creative ideas

How about trying to make a model sailing ship? You could use any available materials – cardboard boxes, cotton reels, pipe cleaners, oddments of this and that.

You could work in groups again if your like. There are some pictures in this book and I'm sure in your library, which would help. Don't forget to paint it. If you make it watertight it might even sail! (See page 28.)

In the doldrums 3rd June 1902

Luck plays a big part in the voyage of a sailing ship. We had sailed about 2,500 miles in 14 days, when suddenly the wind dropped and we were more or less becalmed. The ship scarcely moved at all, and then only if a light breeze sprang up. Such light breezes usually died away as quickly as they had come. We were in the doldrums, near the Equator, and it was terribly hot with no cooling wind. There was little one could do during the day, it was so hot. Some of the older seamen spent some time getting ready or repairing sails – if they could find a bit of shade in which to work!

The nights were cooler – on deck at any rate – and this was the best part of the day for us. One of the older sailors, Ben Gower, would get out his old, wheezy concertina, and we would have a sing-song. Some of the songs were cheery and rollicking, but many were about wives and sweethearts left behind.

Saucy sailor

BOYS
Warmly

1. Come my own one, come my fond one, Come my dear – est, un – to me. Will you wed with a poor sail – or lad, That is just re – turned from sea?

GIRLS

2 O you're dirty, you are ragged,
And your clothes they smell of tar,
So begone, you saucy sailor boy,
So begone you as you are.

BOYS

3 If I'm dirty, if I'm ragged,
And I smell so strong of tar,
Yet I've silver in my pocket
And bright gold I've brought from far.

GIRLS

4 When she heard of his store of gold,
With a smile she then did say
I will wed my saucy sailor boy,
Whom I've loved alway.

BOYS

5 Do you think I am foolish?
Do you think that I am mad?
For to wed a poor country girl,
When there's others to be had.

BOYS

6 So I'll cross the briny ocean,
And when green leaves they do spring,
I will give to another love
This my plain golden ring.

Some accompaniment ideas

RECORDERS OR MELODICAS

Two or three players

Others play the tune.

CHIME BARS OR GLOCKENSPIELS

Three players

TRIANGLES

Play where marked △

Not more than two players.

Play very quietly.

Creative ideas

Make up a four line poem about
a   Your girl (if you are a sailor),
b   Your sailor boy (if you are a girl).
Tell them how much you miss them.

Here are some examples:

From far across the sea,
My thoughts fly home to thee,
Oh Sue, my love, my dearest love,
You are so dear to me.

Sweet Sally Jones I miss you so,
Sally, my Sally,
I think to sea no more I'll go,
Sally, my Sally.

My pillow's wet with tears I've shed,
Johnny my sailor boy,
When you come home let us be wed,
Johnny my sailor boy.

Every night I cry for thee,
Johnny boy, Johnny boy,
Please, oh please come back to me,
My dear Johnny.

Using C D E G A chime bars try to compose a simple tune to fit your words. Use if
possible one note per syllable. You can work in a group if you like.
Teach the song to the class or group. If it's good perhaps you could record it on
tape.

 LISTENING 3

Poll's solo (1)

This piece of music paints a lovely shimmering picture of the sea at night. The
strings of the orchestra are used to make the shimmering sounds. While the **cor
anglais** (a big oboe) and **trumpet** and **horns** add quiet horn calls, see if as you
listen again you can identify the instruments mentioned above. Try to pick them
out from the pictures below. See if you can find other pictures of them in the
library.

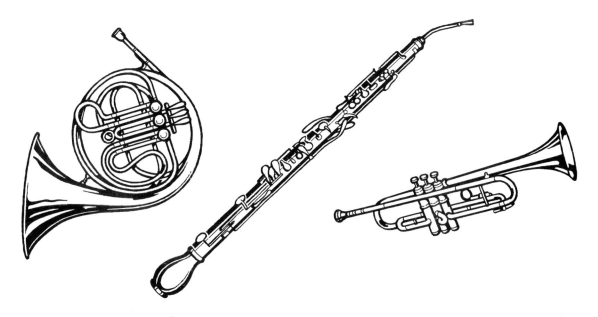

'Salt horse' and dog biscuits
11th June 1902

The food we received during the voyage was very different from what we had had at home, and there was no variety.

The main part of our diet was very hard-baked biscuits called 'Liverpool Pantiles' but known to the sailors as 'dog biscuits'. Before sailing a stock of these pantiles, supposed to be enough for the voyage, was taken on board. As time went by, the biscuits became the home of weevils, and quite often you had to pick the weevils out before eating the biscuit.

Here is what we have to eat every day:

Breakfast – Pantiles soaked in tea and a mug of tea.
Midday Meal – Small piece of salt meat (known as 'salt horse') and pantiles.
Evening Meal – Pantiles and a mug of tea.
On Thursdays and Sundays we had salt pork instead of 'salt horse' and one potato per man – the only fresh vegetables we ever saw.

There was no way of keeping meat or vegetables fresh, and since a lack of fresh vegetables could cause a disease called scurvy, we were given regular drinks of lime-juice.

If food or water – which was carried in tanks – ran short, the captain had to ration the crew. This meant you got even less than you normally would. Captains were under orders not to put into ports for fresh food and water – this would cause delay and expense.

After a hard day's work, it would be wonderful to have some home cooking!

Salt horse

1. Salt horse, salt horse, both near and far, You're food for ev – 'ry hard worked tar; In strong – est brine you have been sunk, Un – til as hard and coarse as junk;[1] To

Faster

eat such tough and wretch – ed fare Would whi – ten e'en a

In time black man's hair, Salt horse, salt horse, **Slower** what brought you here?

2 Salt horse, salt horse, we'd have you know
That to the galley[2] you must go;
The cook without a sign of grief
Will boil you down, and call you beef;
And, we poor sailors standing near,
Must eat you, though you look so queer.
Salt horse, salt horse, what brought you here?

[1] Old rope
[2] The kitchen on board ship

Some accompaniment ideas

This song is best sung unaccompanied, so the instruments can have a rest! Sing the first section down to the word 'junk' *loudly and slowly*. The middle section down to the word 'hair' should be *fast and light*. The end section should be *loud and slow* again.

If you must use an instrument then clash a large cymbal –

once before you begin,
once between the verses, and
once after you've finished.

 LISTENING 4

Poll's solo (2)

Here is the oboe, the small brother of the cor anglais. Hasn't it a lovely, lonely, plaintive sound? It reflects just how we might have felt in the doldrums. Still, quiet, oppressive heat and a little sad in that awful calm stillness.

The music paints that picture so well for us. Perhaps you could find other piece of music among your or the school's records or tapes which have a similar feeling.

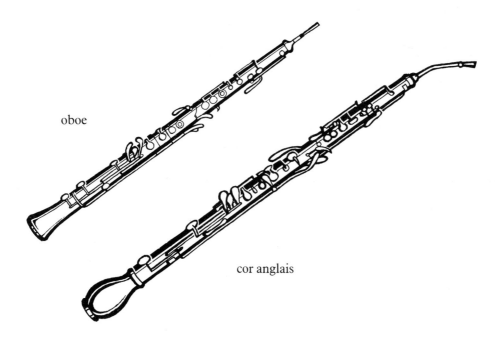

oboe

cor anglais

Creative ideas

Take a recorder – descant or treble – and teach yourself to play the notes.

Using these notes, playing them slowly and smoothly make up a 'doldrum' tune. It will be slow and sad. If you or some of your friends like to dance perhaps they could make up a 'doldrum' dance to your music.

▲ *A ship becalmed in the doldrums*

Cape Horn 25th July 1902

This is our sixth day of gales, and we are still trying to round Cape Horn. I am writing this sitting on top of my sea-chest, with about four inches of icy water splashing round my ankles. I have just come down from the rigging. We were ordered up to furl one of the few sails the ship is still carrying. In the ordinary way, this is not too dangerous, but just now it was a nightmare. The rigging and the yard-arm were coated with ice, my fingers were frozen and the yard-arm was see-sawing. I have never seen such waves in my life – some of them must have been about 50 feet high. How much longer can we go on? The ship is taking a terrible battering and we are all exhausted.

Creative ideas

How about making your own musical storm!
Think about the noises a storm makes – whistling wind, thunder, crashing seas, lightning, rain, roaring sounds, spray.
Get into groups of about ten and try to make appropriate sounds with your body and voices. Your storm will begin far away and gradually get closer and then gradually die away.
Now try adding some percussion instruments. You could use a microphone and a tape recorder for some of the sounds. Use your school tape recorder to help you to hear what the end result is like.

Paddy Doyle's boots

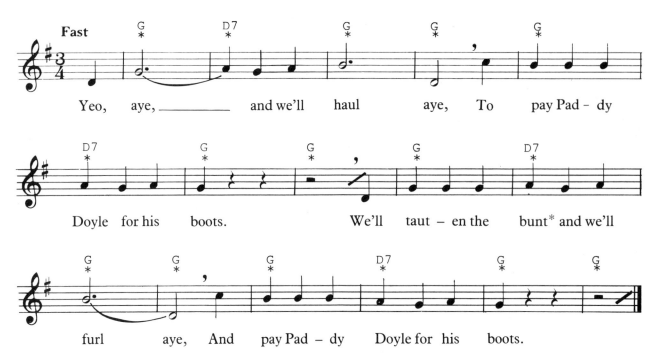

Yeo, aye, ———— and we'll haul aye, To pay Pad - dy

Doyle for his boots. We'll taut – en the bunt* and we'll

furl aye, And pay Pad – dy Doyle for his boots.

2 Yeo, aye, and we'll sing aye,
  To pay Paddy Doyle for his boots.
  We'll bunt up the sail with a fling aye,
  And pay Paddy Doyle for his boots.

* Loose, baggy part of the sail

▼ *Rounding Cape Horn*

Some accompaniment ideas

RECORDER

TAMBOUR (one only)

CHIME BARS OR GLOCKENSPIELS

You only need two chords for this song. Play once as marked on the first beat of
each bar *.

Jasper's solo

As you listen to this music, try to pick out the sounds of the

**solo violin,
harp,
horns.**

Look at the pictures and see if you can tell how these instruments make their sounds?
Draw a picture of each and write down what you do to make it sound.

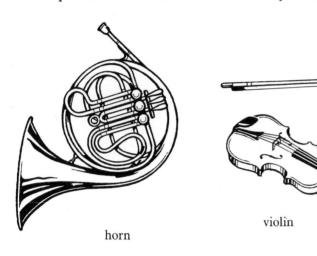

horn

violin

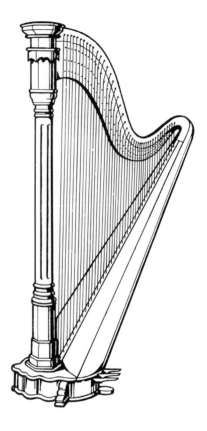

harp

The death of a friend
26th July 1902

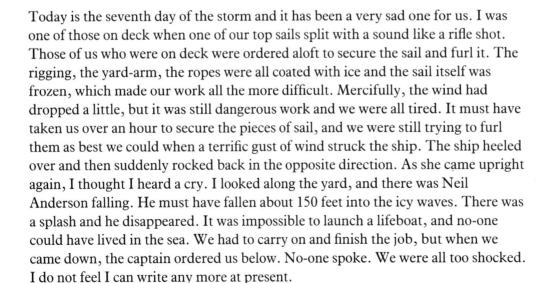

Today is the seventh day of the storm and it has been a very sad one for us. I was one of those on deck when one of our top sails split with a sound like a rifle shot. Those of us who were on deck were ordered aloft to secure the sail and furl it. The rigging, the yard-arm, the ropes were all coated with ice and the sail itself was frozen, which made our work all the more difficult. Mercifully, the wind had dropped a little, but it was still dangerous work and we were all tired. It must have taken us over an hour to secure the pieces of sail, and we were still trying to furl them as best we could when a terrific gust of wind struck the ship. The ship heeled over and then suddenly rocked back in the opposite direction. As she came upright again, I thought I heard a cry. I looked along the yard, and there was Neil Anderson falling. He must have fallen about 150 feet into the icy waves. There was a splash and he disappeared. It was impossible to launch a lifeboat, and no-one could have lived in the sea. We had to carry on and finish the job, but when we came down, the captain ordered us below. No-one spoke. We were all too shocked. I do not feel I can write any more at present.

20

Tom Bowling

Slow and sad

Here a sheer— hulk lies poor Tom Bow – ling, The dar – ling of our

crew. _____ No more he'll hear the tem – pest howl – ing, For

death has broached him to. His form was of the— man – liest beau -ty His

heart was kind— and— soft, _____ Faith – ful be- low Tom did his du – ty, And

now he's gone a – loft_____ And now— he's— gone— a – loft.

2 Tom never from his word departed,
 His virtues were so rare;
 His friends were many, and true hearted,
 His Poll was kind and fair.
 And then he'd sing so blithe and jolly,
 Ah! many's the time and oft;
 But mirth is turned to melancholy,
 For Tom is gone aloft. (*Repeat*)

3 Yet shall poor Tom find pleasant weather,
 When he, who all commands,
 Shall give, to call life's crew together,
 The word to pipe all hands.
 Thus Death, who kings and tars dispatches,
 In vain Tom's life has doff'd;
 For though his body's under hatches,
 His soul is gone aloft. (*Repeat*)

Some accompaniment ideas (for *Tom Bowling*)

Select one or two good recorder players to play the tune. Add a quiet Indian bell-like sound on the first beat of each bar. No other accompaniment is necessary.

 LISTENING 6

Tom Bowling from *Fantasia on British Sea Songs*

This lovely old tune, written by Charles Dibden (an actor, singer who lived in London in 1789) has been arranged by Sir Henry Wood as part of his famous *Fantasia on British Sea Songs*. Listen to the cello play the melody. You could hum the tune quietly as you listen. This music is a regular feature of the 'Last Night of the Proms' in London's Albert Hall.

Sea shanties 19th August 1902

The gales of Cape Horn are behind us, but the memory of Neil Anderson's sad death stays with us. Neil was a quiet, kindly man who hailed from Barra, one of the Western Isles of Scotland. Like so many of the Islanders, he was an excellent seaman, and I for one learned a lot from him.

After the gales around the Horn, and the loss of a good friend, the rest of the voyage has been uneventful. Tomorrow we shall enter the port of Pisagua, in Peru, and Ben Gower, our shanty-man, will be leading us in a capstan shanty as we tie up at the quay. By that time it will be 92 days since the '*Adventurer*' left Cardiff. Had it not been for the tremendous gales around Cape Horn, we would have completed the voyage in a shorter time.

One result of our overlong voyage was that both food and water had to be rationed. I hope the shops in Pisagua have something better to offer than weevilly dog biscuits and rusty-tasting water!

Hullabaloo balay

2 The boarding house was on the quay,
Hullabaloo balay! Hullabaloo balahbalay!
But the lodgers were nearly all at sea.
Hullabaloo balay!

3 A flash young fellow called Shallow Brown,
Hullabaloo balay! Hullabaloo balahbalay!
He followed me mother all round the town.
Hullabaloo balay!

4 Me father said, "Young man me boy",
Hullabaloo balay! Hullabaloo balahbalay!
To which he quickly made reply,
Hullabaloo balay!

5 Next day while dad was in the 'Crown',
Hullabaloo balay! Hullabaloo balahbalay!
Me mother ran off with Shallow Brown.
Hullabaloo balay!

6 Me father slowly pined away,
Hullabaloo balay! Hullabaloo balahbalay!
Cause mother came back on the following day.
Hullabaloo balay!

From *Six Sea Shanties* © Copyright 1925 by Boosey & Company Ltd.
Reprinted by permission of Boosey & Hawkes Music Publishers Ltd.

Some accompaniment ideas

RECORDERS
All play the tune.
A few players could play this:

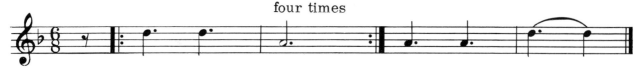

four times

TAMBOURINES
A brisk sharp tap with the knuckles on the first beat of each bar. Those without tambourines could clap again on the first beat of each bar.

CHIME BARS OR GLOCKENSPIEL
Only *one* chord required – D minor.
Play briskly once in each bar on the first beat.
Capture the fun of this song.

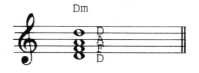

Creative idea

You will have gathered by now that a shanty is a song sung by sailors long ago. Often the solo voice or shanty-man was answered by the others, for example:

SHANTY-MAN   Here we go around the Horn
CREW   Way–hay–oh!
SHANTY-MAN   – – – – – – – – –
CREW   Way–hay–oh!

Using this idea as a pattern, fill in the blanks to make a four-line verse and then write another verse using the same crew line and pattern. Using only three notes (G A E) make up a tune for your verse. Select somebody to be the shanty-man and the rest be the crew. You could pull on imaginary ropes as you sing, or pretend to turn the capstan.
Look at the picture below.

Here are your notes.

Belaye's solo and **Sailor's drill**

1 This music is full of joy and gaiety. It describes exactly how I would feel when my ship turned its nose home. No more 'hard tack' and 'salt horse'! Listen to it once or twice till you can join in and hum the tunes with the orchestra. Can you hear the horns again? Can you pick out the xylophone (hard wooden bars struck with wooden hammers)? Enjoy it!

2 Can you find this tune?

3 Which instrument plays this tune first?

Homeward bound
2nd October 1902

Great news! We sail for home tomorrow! Being in port has been no holiday. First we had to clear our cargo of coal, and that meant days of shovelling. Then we had to repair the damage done by the storms, and the sailmaker was particularly busy, although he had help from various members of the crew, including myself. We had a quick run ashore, but Pisagua is not a very pretty place. However, we did manage to get a square meal! Then came the loading of the cargo for the voyage home. We took on a cargo of nitrate, which is a substance used in making gunpowder.

Now we are almost ready to go. There's a long voyage ahead which includes rounding Cape Horn again, but this time we shall be going home, and that will keep our spirits up. I shall be overjoyed to see my home and my parents again. So tomorrow, it will be 'Good-bye, fare ye well!'

Good-bye, fare ye well

With an easy swing

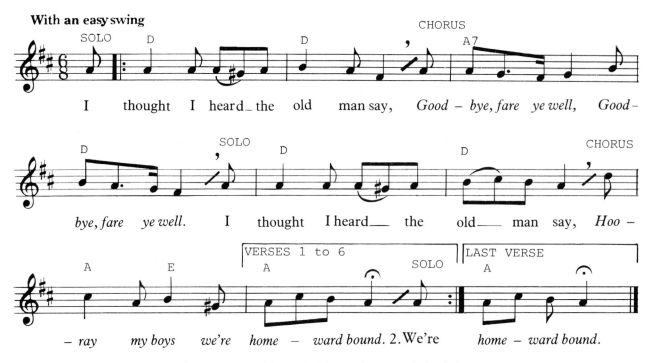

I thought I heard the old man say, *Good – bye, fare ye well, Good-bye, fare ye well.* I thought I heard the old man say, *Hoo – ray my boys we're home – ward bound. 2.We're home – ward bound.*

2 We're homeward bound, I hear the sound. (*twice*)
3 We sailed away to Mobile Bay. (*twice*)
4 But now we're bound for Portsmouth Town. (*twice*)
5 And soon we'll be ashore again. (*twice*)
6 I kissed my Kitty upon the pier

And it's oh to see you again, my dear.
7 We're homeward bound, and I hear the sound. (*twice*)

Some accompaniment ideas

RECORDERS Watch C#!

TRIANGLES Play once on the first beat of each bar.

CHIME BARS

Player 1

CHIME BARS

Player 2

Perhaps you're wondering what became of my great-grandfather. Well, he got round the Horn again all right, for Dad tells us that he spent most of his life at sea. In fact, he became the captain of a steamship. Of course, I never saw him, but now I feel we know quite a lot about him. I hope you enjoyed his stories.

Now I'm going to try to find out as much as I can about the old sailing ships. Maybe you'd like to do the same.

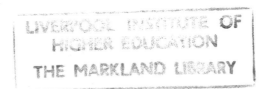

Making a three-masted sailing ship

You will need: An oblong box lid, thin card, pencil, ruler, white paper, scissors, 3mm dowelling (round thin wood from a hobby shop), glue, thread, blu-tack or plasticine, paints.

1 First choose an oblong box lid. Lay down the lid with the top uppermost. Cut 2 strips of card, the same depth and about 3 times the length of the box. Glue the strips to the long sides of the box.

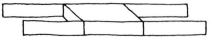

Next bring the strips to a point at one end and fix with glue. Do the same the other end, but first cut the ends to slope like the bow of a ship.

bow

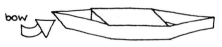

2 To make the deck, place the shape you have made on top of a piece of thin card. Draw round it and then draw 4 tabs at each end for fixing the deck to the hull. Cut out the shape, including the tabs.

Fold down the tabs, glue the deck to the top of your box and the tabs to the inside of the hull. Paint the hull black and the deck brown.

deck

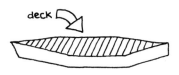

3 Cut 3 pieces of dowelling for the masts. The tallest one should be about half the length of your ship, the other 2 should be shorter. Pierce 3 holes in the part of the deck which covers the box. They should be in line and about the same distance apart. Put in the masts, the tallest in the middle. If they wobble put a small piece of blu-tack or plasticine at the foot of the mast, underneath your ship.

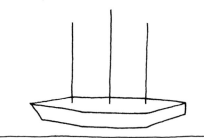

4 Now make 3 sails for each mast. The 2 lower sails on each mast can be the same size. They should be a bit wider than the hull and a little less than a third of the height of the mast. The smallest sail on each mast should be about half the size of the bigger sails. Draw 3 sails for each mast on paper. You might like to give them a curved edge to look as if they are blowing in the wind. Cut them out and glue the middle of each sail to the masts.

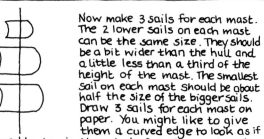

5 Most sailing ships had a foresail of some kind, usually attached by a rope to a round piece of wood called a bowsprit. Use a piece of dowelling a little less than half the size of a mast. Glue half of it to the deck at the bow, then tie or glue a piece of thread from the bowsprit to the top of the first mast.

fold

To make the foresail, cut a triangle shape out of paper. The longest side of the triangle should be the same length as the biggest sail on your ship. Cut it out and then make a small fold along the longest edge. Glue inside the fold, place the fold over the thread and stick together.

6 Your sailing ship is now complete.

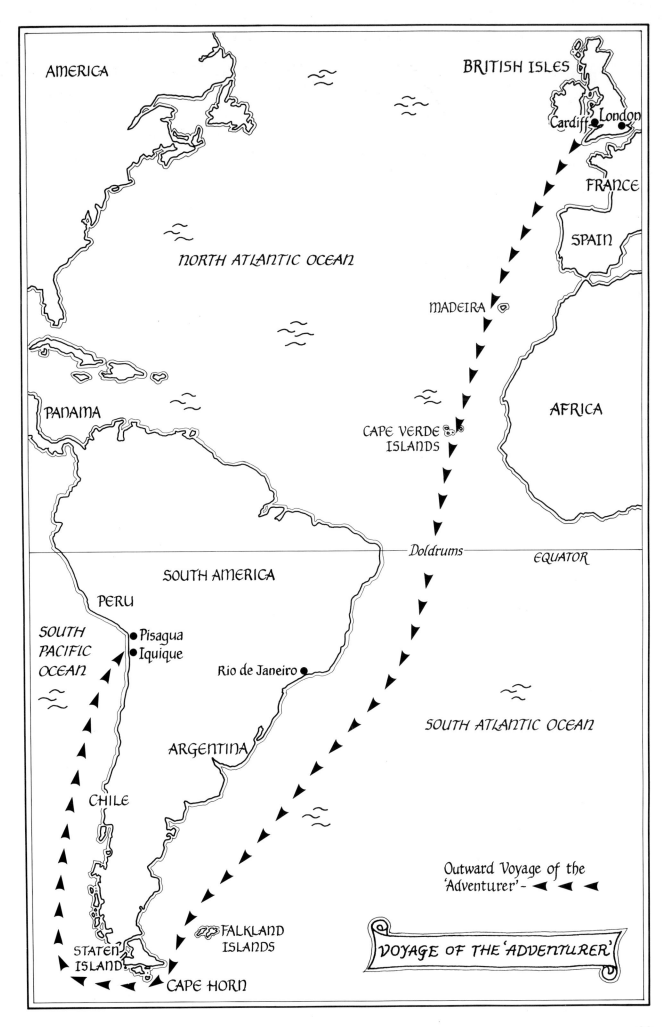

AMERICA

BRITISH ISLES

Cardiff London

FRANCE

SPAIN

NORTH ATLANTIC OCEAN

MADEIRA

AFRICA

PANAMA

CAPE VERDE ISLANDS

Doldrums   EQUATOR

SOUTH AMERICA

PERU

SOUTH PACIFIC OCEAN

Pisagua
Iquique

Rio de Janeiro

SOUTH ATLANTIC OCEAN

ARGENTINA

CHILE

Outward Voyage of the 'Adventurer'—◄ ◄ ◄

FALKLAND ISLANDS

STATEN ISLAND

VOYAGE OF THE 'ADVENTURER'

CAPE HORN

GUITAR CHORD PATTERNS

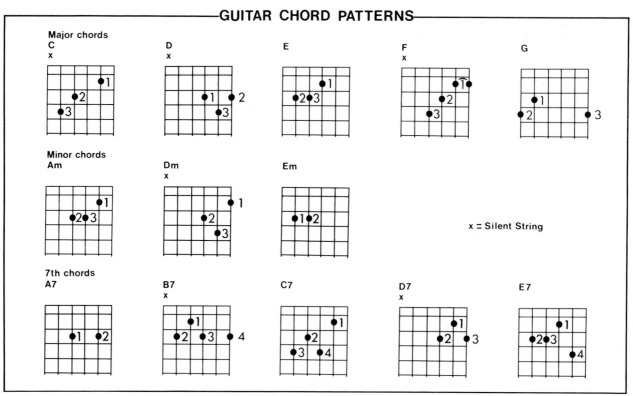

RECORDER NOTES

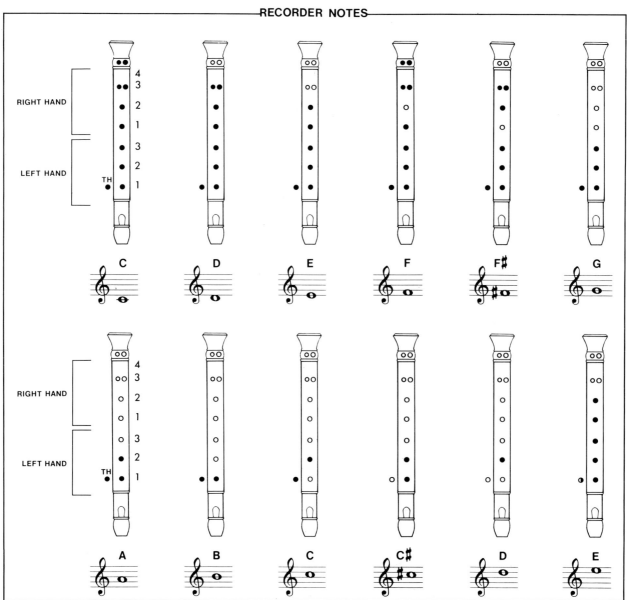

Words to remember

dock: part of a harbour in which ships load and unload.
full-rigged: carrying as many sails as possible.
apprentice: young man who is learning his trade.
bunk: rough bed on board a ship.
ship-shape: tidy; neat and trim.
rigging: the arrangement of ropes on a sailing-ship.
yard: a beam placed across the mast of a sailing ship for spreading square sails.
the sails were broken out: the sails were set.
becalmed: with no wind to move the ship.
doldrums: part of the sea near the Equator where sailing ships were held up for lack of wind.
weevil: a kind of beetle.
scurvy: a disease of the mouth and gums, caused by lack of fresh vegetables; was once very common among sailors.
furl: to roll up.
heel over: to lean on one side.
hatch(es): an opening in the deck of a ship.
under hatches: below deck; off duty.
quay: a landing-place; a place where vessels are loaded and unloaded.

Contents of the cassette

SIDE 1   SONGS (Including teaching versions)

1 Good morning ladies all
2 As off to the South'ard we go
3 Saucy sailor
4 Salt horse
5 Paddy Doyle's boots
6 Tom Bowling
7 Hullabaloo balay
8 Goodbye, fare ye well

Anne Murchie — Soprano
Alexander Wands — Baritone, Guitar
John Wilson — Piano
Ronald Wilson — Engineer

SIDE 2   EXTRACTS

1 Opening dance (scene 1)
2 Jasper's solo (scene 2)
3 Poll's solo (scene 2)
4 Poll's solo (scene 2)
5 Jasper's solo (scene 2)
6 Fantasia on sea songs (Tom Bowling)
7 Belaye's solo and sailor's drill (scene 3)

Extracts 1–5, 7 from *Pineapple Poll*   Royal Philharmonic Orchestra conducted by Sir Charles McKerras
Extract 6   London Symphony Orchestra conducted by Sir Henry Wood

EMI recordings